NEW ZEALAND
style

Peter Murray with Jenna Tartt

OUTDOOR LIVING • FOOD • WINE • RELAXATION AND HOME IDEAS

NEW ZEALAND
style

Murray Books

First published in Australia in 2004 by
Murray Books (Australia)

For distribution in New Zealand by
Whitcoulls Group Ltd

ISBN 0-9580348-1-8

Design and Production: Peter Murray

Our thanks to all those who participated in the making of this book.

A special thank you to Joan Mackenzie for making it possible and Leanne Powell for her valuable insight and assistance.

NEW ZEALAND
style

Peter Murray with Jenna Tartt

Murray Books

NEW ZEALAND
style

inside

10 Lifestyle options

22 Design essentials

26 Beautiful surroundings

30 Coastal lifestyle

40 Interior inspirations

42 Landscape directions

46 The heart of a home

54 Lifestyle and relaxation

56 Untouched World

60 Exploring the far north

64 Relieving the body

66 Inspirational relocation

68 Stress relief

70 Smooth sailing

72 Lifestyle options

90 Interior inspirations

92 Polished style

96 Inspirations - Great home design ideas

130 The food and wine experience – Restaurants, recipes and wines

NEW ZEALAND
style

introduction

New Zealand is a land of diversity, in both its ever changing landscapes and its mix of people and culture. With its clean, green, natural image, beautiful and varied ethnicities, New Zealand offers the perfect lifestyle. With world-class wines and cuisine, awesome landscapes of lush forests and volcanoes, amazing wildlife and a pleasant climate New Zealand is a haven for many outdoor activities, and a great place to unwind. The exciting blend of cultural influences including Maori and Pacific Island, as well as European and Asian creates a diverse, sophisticated, and multicultural blend of people. This unique and dynamic inspiration can be seen in the creativity and artistry of its architects, landscapers and designers and the willingness to experiment. The New Zealand lifestyle is one that no other country could offer. With all of its diverse physical, cultural, and artistic landscapes so close to each other, it is a sanctuary for inspiration – whether it be in the kitchen, home, garden or spare time. This book is a showcase of the lifestyle that New Zealanders enjoy. *New Zealand Style* is a collection of stylish elements including food, wine, interior design, lifestyle, relaxation, the home and garden – everything that makes up our society. Enjoy!

Peter Murray   Jenna Tartt

Lifestyle options

New Zealand home designs over the past decades have always strived to maintain the perfect balance between blending international trends with native designs to organically reflect the beauty of their surroundings. **Contemporary modernism** plays a major role in the city centres, while earthen designs are prevalent in rural areas. Not forgetting perhaps one of the most distinctive eras in modern history, Art Deco too has left its mark on New Zealand. There are wonderful pockets of Deco architecture scattered throughout Auckland's sprawling metropolis, but areas like Napier are famous for it. Napier, redesigned in the Art Deco style after the devastating Hawke's Bay earthquake in 1931, remains filled with a variety and concentration of buildings in Art Deco style that have become an international attraction. One of the most important features of many New Zealand homes is practicality and open planning reflecting our love for the outdoors. Creating a comfortable feel that suits the owner's lifestyle will always remain a key priority – whether that be keeping in the heat or making the most of a scenic view. **The influence of our natural surroundings** can be seen in our love for organic furniture and natural building materials such as stone and wood. Even the most contemporary homes often incorporate natural elements. Both Australia and New Zealand, influenced by their pioneer pasts, use architecture to express the free spirit of a people who are ever-ready to break conventional moulds. From traditional heritage to eye-catching modernism, this part of the world has become a leader in architectural innovation.

Queenstown lifestyle

Over the past decades, it has been realised that New Zealanders tend to be very practical and savvy purchasers who are not flashy by nature. They not only demand excellent design, function, and appeal, but also appreciate honesty and good service. This is certainly true when it comes to real estate. With almost 30 years experience in the industry, Woodlot Properties has been the leading property developer in Queenstown, with an aim to deliver properties far beyond their client's expectations. The family owned and run business has become one of the most trusted and well known developers in New Zealand for this reason. The company is not only involved in property development, but also the real estate market and building design. Teamed with qualified designers and planners, they are able to deliver homes suited to **Queenstown's green environment** while meeting the needs of the local community. Specialising in managing and investing joint venture projects, Woodlot converts vacant land from a conceptual dream into an attainable reality. The sense of space and versatility are important factors when designing houses in New Zealand. The company endeavours to build a strong relationship between the indoors and outdoors of their properties. It is very important to our society as we tend to enjoy our outdoor environment so much, not wanting to close the door on it. We pull inside out, and outside in whenever possible - having the weather determine that balance for us. Privacy is also accentuated in the designs.

To date, New Zealanders have been very fortunate and spoilt for space. With this space naturally comes privacy, therefore it is important to create the perfect balance in designing open planned living spaces while maintaining privacy and enough isolation from other developments. **Organic architecture** is important as the properties are usually set in picturesque locations full of natural beauty. While attempting to camouflage into the surroundings the houses are designed to incorporate the natural landscape. Woodlot Properties are fortunate to have the most scenically wonderful natural canvas to design against and they wish to enhance this, **not inhibit the natural beauty of their surroundings**. By using natural materials and earthen colours the developments are able to blend harmoniously with the mountains and forests of Queenstown. There is plenty of room inside the houses for diversity and colour. The company began by initially focusing on the workforce market, as the Founder and Managing Director, David Broomfield, felt that this was where the heart and future of the community rested. From there, other market opportunities grew and now the company provides a range of properties for equally varying budgets. Because the company is family owned and run, there is a definite long-term focus on property development in the Queenstown area.

Alpenrose

Alpenrose, a six villa development, sits proudly on the hill overlooking Lake Wakatipu and the township of Queenstown, where shops and restaurants are only minutes away. With sweeping vistas of Cecil, Walter and Bobs Peaks, the Remarkables and Kelvin Heights and its golf course, each villa is designed to take advantage of these views, which are some of Queenstown's most spectacular. Each villa has central to its living area an open fire, bordered by large glass doors allowing open-plan space to flow freely onto an expansive deck overlooking the lake. The clean-lined kitchen, incorporates modern appliances, with large working surfaces. Each villa has three or four spacious bedrooms - the master bedroom containing an extravagant walk-in-wardrobe and ensuite, with double basins, spa bath, toilet and a double shower. This bedroom, along with the second one, opens out onto other individual viewing decks. The garage sizing is generous, providing bays for two cars with space along side for storage, or a moderate sized boat. The concept of this development was to take the classic New Zealand 1950's bach and give it a fresh modern flavour. With a blend of weather board, plaster, glass and rock, the design is a contemporary version of something we all know and love. The interiors are a mix of warmth and luxury, allowing you to feel at home, while inviting in some of Queenstown's grandest views.

Grand View

This development is on the very sunny and sought-after Tucker Beach Road, Queenstown. These properties are fresh on the market, with newly formed building sites, sealed access and feature entrance. They boast some of the most spectacular rural and river views in the district, with northerly outlooks over the Shotover River and Coronet Peak.

The two level home features 4 bedrooms, 4 bathrooms (3 ensuites), rock chimney - open fire, central heating throughout, Fisher & Paykel Iridium range (easy clean stainless steel) including extractor, dishdrawers, gas oven and cook top. Double glazed windows, an open planned kitchen and dining area with large wooden sliding doors into living area is a main feature. Outside living with landscaping is ideal for modern living.

Closeburn station

Closeburn Station offers the unique
opportunity to buy into New Zealand's rich
rural heritage. Surrounded by native flora,
fauna and wildlife this breathtaking lakeside
property, offers the first true life-style
residential investment within a working high
country station and situated 11 km from the
international scenic resort of Queenstown. The
27 freehold titles to building sites include a
1/27 share in the station, a club house/barn,
tennis court, fishing lodge and three mountain
huts. The surrounding natural scenery is
spectacular. The battle of "Aemon Hen" was
filmed on this site. Closeburn station
encompasses three mountain lakes making the
scope of recreational activities quite
unsurpassed.

Design essentials

Purple South, boasting world famous furniture designers David Trubridge and Werner Aisslinger (right) in their working group, have been inspired by **the New Zealand way of life** so entirely that their main drive is to share this style with the world. The furniture designed and created by the company is oceanic in mood, borrowing from the ancient ways of the Maori and their relationships with the sea. The Punakaiki Rocks, located at New Zealand's untamed West Coast, and the simple brilliance of traditional Maori canoes can be seen in Aisslinger's collection of furniture consisting of interlocking elements that offer stunning details while being highly practical to transport. International shooting star David Trubridge got involved with Purple South in 2003. His contribution to the Purple South range 'Glide' is a wonderful rocking recliner from steam bent Ash that reflects his interest in indigenous design of sailing vessels and other structures for survival. Based in Auckland, the company was founded in 2002 by New Zealander Amanda Hookham, a successful interior designer, known through the British / New Zealand TV - Programme Changing Rooms and by Oliver Kraft, head of the Vitra Design Museum's educative department, and author of TV - documentary films on design, before his migration to New Zealand. In July 2003, after an exciting time of research and prototyping, Purple South launched their first range in New Zealand and shortly after in Australia. The range is now also available in Europe after a very successful launch during the Milan furniture fair in April 2004. Purple South try to capture the spirit of New Zealand and allow others, in Europe, Australia and the USA to understand and feel the beauty of this paradise.

New Zealand is a wild place, full of natural beauty and nature, from the mountains, oceans, great lakes, forests and tropical areas it is like no where else in the world. Purple South want to share the exoticness and untouched spirit of this place with others. The youth of the country, free from the restraints history places on many locations in Europe, also creates a more accepting society and one that is willing to experiment. The Purple South designs offer beauty and art, as well as being functional. It is a combination of cultures that allows them to be influenced by so many different things. In New Zealand there may be a street with more than 170 nationalites residing there. New Zealanders are not afraid to mix things up and we reflect this in our furniture. **The label is proud of manufacturing nuclear free** with materials from sustainable resources and believes that in a product-flooded world, their furniture needs to be unique, beautiful, transport emotions and offer more than functionality. The company began with the inspiration found in a suitcase filled with 'Kiwiana', hundreds of objects representing New Zealand from Manuka oils and bush honey to contemporary New Zealand music. The suitcase that travels from town to town and country to country to fulfil its mission just returned with brand new ideas for table ware from Dutch designer Ed Annink and is currently on its way to inspire Paris based British designer Matt Sindall. As they are only in the early stages of establishment, Purple South believe that they are yet to gain full trust from the New Zealand market, but are sure this will come in time. The New Zealand market is still very driven by imports and the mentality that international products are better. This is slowly changing and people are becoming proud of the products that come from their country. There is so much excellent work coming out of New Zealand, with art and design especially.

Beautiful surroundings

The magical feeling of dipping into a pool in your own personal oasis is a sensation that few things surpass. Whether it is a large family pool or a spa for two, a pool can add the finishing touches to any home. With busy lifestyles and hectic schedules, your own pool can also be the perfect place for recreation and exercise with friends and family. It can be safely said that few cultures place **the emphasis on family**, health and outdoor living as we do in New Zealand – and a pool can enhance the qualities of each of these factors. As the pressures of other aspects of our lives continue to increase, the ease and accessibility of being able to relax and exercise in your own beautiful surroundings at home has become paramount. Mayfair Pools are widely acclaimed throughout New Zealand and the South Pacific region for their award winning designs and superior construction techniques which are built to last. Their unique system of swimming pool construction is designed to withstand the problems caused by frequent earthquakes and ground movement prevalent in most areas of New Zealand. The patented method ensures adherence to engineering and council requirements warranting a long lasting design that will stay strong throughout the years. Pool designs have blossomed over the past years and can be integrated to enhance every backyard and lifestyle. Mayfair Pool builders are also specialists in repairing and remodelling existing swimming pools, offering the sensible solution to renovating and modernising an ageing pool. Colour, shape and design can be changed with novel water features added. Using unique edging, stepping and lighting are just some of the elements which can enhance pool landscape. Heating and swim jets can also be added to increase the enjoyment and use of the pool year-round.

Pool design and landscaping are much more sophisticated than they once were; a pool is now seen as an extension of a house or garden and is designed accordingly. The use of solar heating and fibre-optic lighting now means that pools can be used year round - day or night. A pool should reflect the style of its house and garden. Pools set out in the yard should have a more natural setting with well-blended finishes, while pools close to the house may need to have a more distinctive design and finish to match the lines of the house.

Coastal lifestyle

The rugged coastline and endless oceans surrounding New Zealand are a continual source of inspiration for architects Tim Nees and Justin Wright. Founding New Work Studios in 1993, Tim has always been influenced by the strength of structure and the beauty of the raw materials sculpted by nature. NWS beachside designs are always created to coincide with the beauty of the foreshore. The aesthetics and effectiveness of the materials found on a beach interests them in many ways. Based in Wellington, when NWS first opened it was a combined art and design studio. This continues to influence the creativeness and originality of the architectural designs they produce today. The winner of 14 New Zealand Institute of Architects awards over the past 6 years, the company mainly focuses on high quality residential projects and recently venturing into hospitality design. Their current work includes new homes, townhouse developments, luxury motels, bars, taverns winery cellars and smaller residential alterations. A mixture of natural materials, recycled products and modern designs **creates an interesting appeal** and one that is unique to NWS. Objects such as recycled oregon beams and old weatherboards give a sense of distinct character and heritage while materials such as rock and driftwood connect with nature. NWS also specialises in renovations to completed houses, adding value and appeal to any property. Their distinctive style can be observed in all of their projects, creating matchless charm through their use of textures and different organic materials.

Right: The main living space is viewed through open sliding doors. A mixture of robust and smooth surfaces - honed concrete floor, large in situ concrete fireplace, recycled oregan beams and posts, customwood linings, hanging light panels, plywood joinery.

Ranger Point

"We do have unique ideas, but people approach us knowing that and liking that. A lot of clients come to us asking for distinctive ideas. We do a lot of renovations and transform older houses into something completely different, something original" says Tim. Tim and Justin say that most of the time all their clients desire is a comfortable living area that is attractive yet still affordable. This is particularly achievable with renovations and the use of recycled materials. The Ranger Point house uses supplies from a variety of found objects and materials which refer to the site and the exposed **southern coastal setting**. New Zealand not only offers a unique location filled with lots of natural local materials, but also an eclectic mix of cultures and ideas that help create a very modern and distinctive style. It is a unique place, a small island where people from different countries have been placed together to create their own new culture. The people here are interested in buildings that are more than just timber and bricks. The character of the newer homes here is different to anywhere else. Adding to this creative resource of ideas is NWS wide range of active imaginations. The Studio originally combined an art gallery with an architectural firm. Compiling contemporary New Zealand art from a range of leading local artists with talented architects led to a ministry of original ideas. NWS are inspired by the way things are put together to create a particular ambience. They are always looking at ideas from overseas or different cultures and bring those aspects into their work.

The forms and materials form a bricolage of found objects and materials which refer to the site and the exposed southern coastal setting. The old weatherboards with peeling paint were recycled from the old house which previously occupied the site. Other claddings are rusted steel sheet, stained plywood and translucent white plastic.

Right: a double height entry space with stair rising to upper level. The stairs are recycled jarrah treads and stringers, hoop pine ply balustrade with steel balusters. The large wall features contemporary NZ art. The walls re lined with grooved customwood panels.

Ranger Point

Left: The bathroom features an old cast iron bath, with corrugated baby iron and rusted steel sheet wall linings around the shower. The flooring is a fibreglass roofing membrane.

Below: Exterior view from the tennis court to the new extension at dusk. This project was an alteration and extension to a 1970's beachside cottage. The beachside front of the house was demolished and replaced by a new wing incorporating a verandah and outdoor room. Right: Because the house is exposed to strong off shore winds, the verandah is protected by a series of sliding timber screens. The house itself has also been clad in the fine cedar slats and all exposed framing is Lawson Cypress timber left to weather naturally. A tennis court sits between the house and the beach.

Tahiti Bay

Right: An evening view from shore across the road at a home at Palmer Bay. An extreme makeover on an old cottage, a new upper storey was added, housing bedrooms and bathrooms, and the existing lower floor was opened up to the coastal environment with an enlarged living space. The upper floor is clad in recycled oregan timber boards in a random pattern.

Palmer Bay

Right: The new stairs and display shelves. The owner has a collection on 1960's ceramic McAlpine fridge jugs which needed displaying. The stairs are laminated meranti veneer plywood and steel. A skylight brings light from above into the back of the living room.

Left: The new bathroom upstairs has views from the bath and shower of the coast and sea. Imagine lying back and watching the ships sail past. This stretch of water is the entry into Wellington harbour from the Cook Strait.

Interior inspiration - fabrics

The new Langdon House collection from Studio brings warmth and feeling long absent from the contemporary home back to its rightful position. The range introduces a fresh palette of soft, soothing colours and traditionally based patterns that invite intimacy and formality; Langdon House envelopes the interior with a modern yet familiar look perfect for the home. The vast, opulent interiors of an Italian palazzo or an English manor are echoed in the stunning collection including beautiful moiré background and pocket weave constructions that lend an air of fine quality and sophistication to any interior space. The soft gold of Amesbury and Monticello resonate with lyrical musings of the baroque while the lush cranberry of Jefferson and Langdon House and the delectable olive of Lamberton and Cello, add a tantalizing soupçon of grace and style. Studio has designed a magnificent decorative collection of coordinated patterns and weaves, tiebacks and tassels, where modern colours merge with traditional styles to create a harmonious ambience of refined family living.

Landscape directions

Because of its ideal climatic conditions, New Zealand is the perfect place to design and create gardens Vegetation grows faster here than in many other places, and a wide range of plants can be used because of the diverse landscapes and regions. Garden designs vary all over the country, with large acreage in most rural areas to small courtyards in the city centres. Because of this, layout and plant choice are important factors in designing your garden. Dietmar Bostfleisch, the Director and Principal Landscape Architect of the Studio of Landscape Architecture, believes that the **garden should be an extension of the house**, harmoniously designed to incorporate the features of the home. A close relationship between architecture and landscape architecture is a vital feature to guarantee an outstanding design. It is important that the garden is part of the living areas. The idea is to create an area which is inviting, practical and unique – an extension of the home. Dietmar suggests that gardens should not only be extensions of their correlating houses, but also the surrounding environment. Stunning native plants such as the Silver Fern, as well as the Nikau palm and Cabbage Tree are beautiful alternatives to exotic species. Though many introduced plants thrive in New Zealand, it is important to utilise the wide variety of native plants. Studio of Landscape Architecture also emphasises the importance of individuality. The innovation and success of the designs are reflected in the unique identity of each project. This is because the specific needs for the individual client is of primary importance.

Originally from Berlin, Dietmar has been in the industry for 16 years and bases the principles of his company on the tradition and background of his experience in Europe and New Zealand. "A very positive aspect of operating in New Zealand is that you see the results of your vision in a relatively short period of time. Plants grow significantly faster than in Europe and the Landscape Architect's vision is realised within years not decades as is the case in other parts of the world" he says. The huge variety of landscapes makes New Zealand an interesting place to garden, from the tropical north with its palms and broadleaf trees to the mountains with their alpines, tussock and grasses. **The abundant coastlines of New Zealand** can also create a challenge for gardeners, but with some of the most stunning results. As more and more of us have smaller, even courtyard, gardens today, the choices we make to utilise our green space becomes more significant. City gardens are becoming smaller and smaller but if well designed they do add significant value to the property and create character within the home. The value and appreciation of Landscape architecture is beginning to be realised as it can add dramatically to the value of a property and it ensures the best utilisation of the **outdoor living and entertaining areas**. What we do has enduring impact and influence on the environment, both structural and natural, as well as on those who form part of it through living, working or playing. We should have a professional commitment to creating open spaces that improve, enhance and contribute to our culture and our community.

The heart of a home

On a cold winter's night, there is nothing like the glowing warmth of a fireplace to create the feeling of homely comfort. For centuries the fireplace has been the traditional gathering place of any home, and once again the trend is returning in modern and innovative designs. With new technology it is possible to have the beauty and magic of the open fireplace combined with heat efficiency and ease of use. Today's fireplaces are not only economically efficient and easy to maintain, but are **no longer limited to the central living** area of the home. Modern designs and a growing desire for alfresco living have seen fireplaces migrate from the lounge and dining areas out onto the patios or pool surroundings. Whether it is a pleasant summer's evening or a cool winter's day, an outdoor fireplace introduces a warm ambience to any outdoor dining occasion. There is now a wide range of both outdoor and indoor fireplaces in various sizes that can be customised to suit any living area available. Whether wood, gas-burning or electric, a fireplace can be installed new or retro-fitted into an existing chimney. The fireplace is now **the heart of a home**, a focal point for people to gather around and enjoy each others company. In order to achieve these principles, design, décor, ambience, warmth and comfort must be the overriding factors. To truly appreciate the magic of an open fire, one must experience it in every sense – the feeling of warmth, the enchantment of dancing flames, the relaxing sounds and smells. It is this complete experience that no other form of heating could ever attain.

Winter is no reason to abandon the enjoyment of alfresco living, gathering around an outdoor fireplace is a great way to relax with friends and family.

These days it is possible to have it all - the beauty of an open fireplace combined with an efficient heat source.

Whether catering for new home installations, retro-fitting into an existing masonry fireplace or outdoor situations, you are now able to match and create innovative solutions for any situation using wood, gas or electric fireplaces.

Lifestyle and relaxation

Though relaxation has always been an enjoyable part of living in New Zealand, it has also become an important part of life as well. With growing stresses of everyday life, **it is vital to find time to spend relaxing** and enjoying the life we live on our island paradise. New Zealanders can enjoy every variety of sporting and leisure activity you'd care to imagine, and with around 15,000 kilometres of coastline, it is little wonder we love relaxing in the water. We have always had an enthusiasm for ocean-going craft, remaining at the forefront of yacht design and racing during much of the 20th century, and continuing our dominance into this century by winning and retaining the prestigious America's Cup. Sailing is a common pastime and one that anyone can enjoy, whether being chartered by professionals or venturing out on your own. Going to the beach, swimming, surfing, whale watching, sailing and windsurfing are all valuable ways to unwind. With New Zealand's non-stop parade of beautiful beaches often the most relaxing activity is to sit on the shore and breathe the sea-scented air while you enjoy a view that changes slowly with the tide. Hot springs are another **source of quiet repose**. From Waiwera in the north to Welcome Flat in the south, geothermic heated water provides many opportunities to lie back and take it easy. These natural hot mineral baths around volcanic areas are perfect for relaxing muscles and relieving tension. For thousands of years Polynesians have bathed in these remedial baths to improve muscle development and cure aches and pains. The alleviating affect of hot water bathing and other therapeutic activities can also be easily achieved in city centres, far from the volcanoes of Rotorua or Taupo. Day spas and relaxation centres are the contemporary way of attaining inner peace and harmony.

Untouched World

New Zealand comprises of the **most beautiful landscapes** in the world. With plants and animals that occur no where else, it is important that we preserve the natural wonder of our country. This is why environment sustainability and renewal is the focus of the New Zealand lifestyle brand Untouched World. Peri Drysdale, founder and Chief Executive Officer of Snowy Peak Limited, formed Untouched World in 1998 as a vehicle to influence attitudes towards the environment through fashion. She believes that fashion is a powerful medium for change and has the capacity to shake inherent complacency about the environment felt in today's societies. Their vision is to help people recognise what is possible for people and the planet. The eco-conscious and globally aware label symbolises much that is valued by New Zealanders - nature and the outdoors united with comfort and style. Combining high quality design and function, the garments are perfect for emphasising **the very essence of New Zealand lifestyles** where freedom, adventure, harmony with nature and a life enriched by multi-cultural heritage can co-exist. The innovative fabrics are easy to care for, ideal for travelling and designed to travel freely between soft outdoor adventures through the oval office to the elegant restaurant. Original fabrics used include 'Mountainsilk', which is 100 percent pure, fine merino wool, for which our country is renowned. With its high crimp levels packed densely together, the fabric protects the wearer from the hot desert sun to the coldest nights of the high alpine areas. The 'Merinomink' range is an innovation that combines the fur of the feral possum with merino wool. The result is a durable, light, soft and warm fabric.

The main goal is to lead the change in attitudes toward environmental sustainability. They feel that it is important to raise awareness that there are better options, not only for the environment but for the population. Untouched World does not only offer the finest fashion garments, but a whole range of environmentally friendly products such as its face and body range as well as jewellery. A visit to Untouched World is a total retail experience. There is a restaurant, an art gallery and even treks available through the Walter Peak Experience. **Untouched World's Walter Peak Treks** are an opportunity for small groups of two to six people to explore some of the 67,000 acres of dramatic remote country otherwise seen only by sheep and musterers. It is a rugged three day guided experience staying in genuine mustering huts and you are served gourmet food each night. The Untouched World Foundation is yet another arm of the company, established to support and positively enhance the philosophies of the brand. The foundation undertakes projects that provide focal points to allow the company to directly and indirectly make the most positive overall impact on the future of our planet and its people. This is effectively done through education and promotion of social, cultural and community issues. Snowy Peak has received multiple awards. In 1992 Peri Drysdale was made a Member of the Order of the British Empire (MBE) for services to New Zealand (Manufacturing and Export), and in 1999 received a North and South award for being one of 100 New Zealanders making largest contributions to New Zealand, the last year of the millennium. Her dedication to her company and its plight saw her win 2002 Business Woman of The Year.

Exploring the far north

You do not have to go far to enjoy tropical paradise in New Zealand, the Bay of Islands region has a world class maritime park with spectacular weather. The region hosts 144 Islands and secluded bays, combined with its tranquil pace and the endless offerings of holiday activities it is the perfect place to unwind. The Bays pristine natural environment is the gathering place in the South Pacific for overseas sailing yachts on world cruises, international sport fishermen, golfers and marine enthusiasts. The perfect way to enjoy such an environment is to relax for a few days in a local beach front lodge. Situated on the Marlin Coast in the north of the Bay of Islands is the **Cavalli Beach House Retreat**, a stylish architecturally designed lodge that enjoys a reputation as one of the few absolute beachfront properties in New Zealand. Only a four hour drive from Auckland or a 45 minute flight, it is the perfect weekend getaway. Nestled in its own private bay just 20 metres from the shoreline the Beach House comprises three luxurious guest accommodation areas. Each room has a large balcony with magnificent, wide and uninterrupted ocean views, perfect for dining al fresco or enjoying the sun's rays. The in-house cuisine is a celebrated feature of the lodge with the freshest seasonal produce and home-grown salad greens and herbs – a New Zealand wine list offers a selection of medal-winning wines. The retreat has an abundance of fresh seafood and grow their our own vegetables and herbs. You couldn't get any fresher – it comes straight from the ocean or the garden and onto your plate. Combine the highest quality meat and a brilliant chef and you have a perfect meal.

Full days can be spent sampling the many attractions in the area, leaving no shortage of activities to enjoy. To the north snorkelling and diving can be experienced in the beautiful bays and on the west coast the giant kauris trees of the Waipoua Kauri Forest can be explored. Skippered yachting, deep-sea fishing, line fishing and scenic charters are all available along the beautiful Whangaroa Harbour and the Marlin Coast. The north-east coast of New Zealand is **world-famous for its big game fishing grounds** with some of the largest marlins recorded being caught off the Bay of Islands. For those interested in snorkelling and diving, world class diving charters are available including the underwater exploration of the Greenpeace flagship 'Rainbow Warrior' sunk at the Cavalli Islands. There is everything from deep sea fishing to yachting, but for those who want a more relaxing break they also have a masseuse, spa pool, hairdresser and beauty therapist. The Far North is an area full of artisans with a large variety of arts and crafts available for viewing and sale. The region has a wide variety of cafes and restaurants suited to all palates and budgets, many boasting award-winning venues. At the many art and craft shops in Kerikeri, you will find high quality goods made and sold on the premises.

Relieving the body

New Zealand's volcanoes are not only the source of its large mountains, geysers, mud pools and volcanic valleys, but also for the natural hot mineral pools located in areas such as Rotorua. The benefits of bathing in hot mineral pools have been known to our ancestors for hundreds of years. Spa development in Rotorua exists because of the natural abundance of hot mineral water that flows from the earth's thin crust in this actively volcanic area of New Zealand. If used regularly, the health benefits of mineral bathing include preventative and curative measures against arthritis and rheumatism, also relaxing the body and relieving weekly stress. However, as a one off experience it is also valuable as an unbeaten source of stress relief and muscle relaxation. The Polynesian Spa in Rotorua offers this unique form of relaxation to the many hundreds of thousands of clients it hosts every year. Many stop by for a solitary visit while passing through, however the 500 local members who go there daily believe they are reaping the real benefits. Distinctive therapies include Aix therapy or 'Aix Les Bains', originating from France and introduced to the area in the early 1900s. This massage involves being massaged by jets of hot mineral water while being rubbed with coconut oil. The combination of the two elements creates an extremely effective hydrotherapy massage, beneficial for circulation and relaxation. Other therapies offered by the spa involve natural New Zealand products such as mineral filled Rotorua mud and Manuka honey, which possesses skin healing properties. The Lake Spa Retreat is Polynesian Spa's deluxe bathing and relaxation haven comprising four shallow rock-pools of varying temperatures (36C to 43C), set in a New Zealand bush environment overlooking Lake Rotorua.

Inspirational relocation

In 1995 a short holiday at Lake Taupo changed the lives of John and Ruth Boddy forever. When the owners of a dairy farm visited the region, it was wet and cold, so the couple decided to fill in time looking at big houses that were for sale. They fell in love with a picturesque mansion and gave up their old lifestyles, opting for a life as owners of the boutique bed and breakfast. Much work was done to the three acres surrounding the home, resulting in **a beautiful and relaxing space** with scenery rivalling the finest resorts. A hill was removed to accommodate the tennis court, a swimming pool was built and many trees were planted, including the pillar trees fronting the property which the mansion was named after. Often described as the jewel in the crown of New Zealand's north island, Taupo is a vibrant place, filled with fresh air, rivers, lakes and scenic opportunities. The town of Taupo is set amidst many lakes and rivers, green countryside, **spectacular mountain scenery**, beautiful native bush and some of the largest pine forests in the Southern Hemisphere. The area's lakes and rivers are very popular for a variety of both winter and summer water sports, including sailing, water skiing and jet boating. Its neighbouring countryside provides the perfect environment for a number of land sports, including mountain biking and hiking. The region has long been known as the trout fishing capital of the world, offering some of the best angling in New Zealand for rainbow and brown trout, in both the lake and its two major rivers – the Tongariro and the Waikato. Taupo is also ideally located just a short drive from Mt Ruapehu and Whakapapa skifield – **the largest ski area in New Zealand** – offering a variety of runs perfect for both skiing and snow boarding at a beginners to advanced level.

Stress relief

New Zealand is a melting pot of cultures from around the world, and influences from every continent can be seen here in everyday life. One of the benefits of this is the assembling of the best treatments and products. The perfect example can be found in l'unova Medi-spa. A truly European experience, l'unova offers complete relaxation and beauty treatments with exclusive products unavailable elsewhere in New Zealand. Located in Auckland, the Medi spa dedicates itself to stress relief and enhancing **the natural beauty of the human body**. The combination of the latest non-surgical beauty techniques and traditional relaxation therapies achieves a sensual and holistic approach to your wellbeing. Living with a sense of vitality and youthfulness is something we all want to maintain. The spa is the only spa in Auckland to cleverly combine traditional spa treatments with a state-of-the-art cosmeceutical range of beauty and body products and treatments to guarantee visible results. Rich in concentrated, frozen cellular extracts, Ericson Laboratoire skin care is fast becoming the treatment of the 21st century, when it comes to effective, non-surgical face lifts, anti aging and anti cellulite treatments. New Zealand women are seeing the results and realising that for perfect skin you have to work at it, just as you would with anything. The spa does not only offer beauty therapies, but also relaxation massages and aromatherapy as part of their **holistic approach to beauty and wellbeing**. The spa is specially designed so that the minute you walk through the doors you enter a unique tranquil setting, soothing away the stresses of every day life through aromatherapy and serene settings.

Smooth sailing

New Zealand's passion for yachting and love affair with the ocean have been the catalyst for its world-class marine industry. The industry's export success is built on excellence in yacht design and construction as well as proven success in **world class sporting events**. Fuelled by his passion for sailing and believing that he had the necessary skills, Peter White-Robinson opened a super yacht construction company after New Zealand's success at the San Diego America's Cup in the mid-1990s. The first super yacht completed by the company was the Spirit of Fitzroy – a vision made real. The 25 metre, Alan Warick designed pilot-house cruiser, has become the company's flagship and was launched early in 2000 to coincide with New Zealand's successful defence of the America's Cup. Spirit of Fitzroy met with immediate acclaim from the international boating community for the quality of workmanship and finish evident in the vessel. Peter, who grew up on the shores of Tonga has always had an affinity with the ocean, but never imagined he could be doing what he does today. With a love of yachting and water, his career has been too good to be true. He also believes that **New Zealand is the perfect place** for a yachting company as the island is surrounded by vast oceans and the people are passionate about boating. New Plymouth is also a particularly appropriate setting as it is the head of the New Zealand engineering industry. Set in the heart of Taranaki, New Plymouth offers a wealth of activities and facilities all within a few kilometres of each other. Towering over the entire region is the 2,518 metre high Mount Taranaki, New Zealand's most accessible alpine area. Attracting over 300,000 visitors annually for the superb skiing, tramping and mountaineering, it is complemented by amazing views and scenery. It is the ideal place to be, good business, beautiful environment, mountains, oceans, parks and foreshore – it's all here.

Lifestyle options

Many elements are combined in the recipe of developing your own dream home, the key ingredient being the perfect house design. It is important that all factors are attended to including comfort, practicality, character and style. Leading New Zealand architect Don Nelson considers these factors to be essential and each house is carefully designed to reflect the owners' lifestyle. The mixture of contemporary New Zealand ideas with **Mediterranean influences** has resulted in the company designing some of the most impressive work in the country. Simple, modern forms are teamed with asymmetrically placed windows, doors and arcades to create lots of wide, spacious living areas. Usually comprising of free-flowing curves and extensive use of outdoor living areas, the homes are well-suited to New Zealand's mild climate and relaxed, family-orientated lifestyle. The designers also understand that another important element to any house is the dressing of the grounds. Landscaping is not overlooked and most times bold natives such as pohutukawa trees are used to accentuate the New Zealand feel and provide plenty of shade to keep the house cool during summer months. These accentuated garden designs add character and complement the confident house designs. Each landscape is different, designed in relation to the site of the house and to be complementary to the surrounding areas as well as providing an attractive finish to the **alfresco living spaces**.

Influenced by the site's native vegetation and proximity to the ocean, the house is distinctively Mediterranean. Bifold doors open the house to expansive patios and gardens creating perfect spaces for alfresco living.

To make the most of the home's scenic beachfront location, the kitchen and family room feature curved glass windows providing views from all angles. The main living areas flow onto patios and the swimming pool via bifold doors. Wide eaves, along with the statuesque pohutukawa trees, provide plenty of shade and keep the house cool during summer months.

Sweeping curves are apparent in both the interior and exterior walls. The interior columns create height and a sense of grandeur.

Landscaping around the new home should accommodate and accentuate the location of the house. Here, palms, succulents and hardy native shrubs were chosen to complement the Mediterranean style of the design and provide an attractive finish to the outdoor living areas.

Every area of the house is lit by the large internal skylight which is the main feature of the home. Cool colours have been used throughout to blend with the dark tones of the furniture and timber stairs.

The perfect site for the dream home. The
views are captured with the use of large
openings that are closed off at night by
cafe doors. The inside blends with
outdoors easily with the use of lush pot
plants both inside and out.

The lighting and open living areas compliment the new landscaping, demonstrating the high level of architectural detailing that is required in every new home.

Curved bands have expanded the home, with wide bifold doors opening onto the covered outdoor dining area. The balcony can be accessed from several parts of the house enhancing the home's flow of indoor/outdoor living spaces.

Interior inspiration - paint

Perfect Blues – Spring Rain

Brighten up your interior by using beautiful blues. Blues are so calming to live with and can give you a very welcoming feeling. We have used Dulux Dolphin Daze in this living space to give out a very peaceful and comforting effect. To create a contrasting colour scheme we have added Dulux Sandshoe for the trims and shelving unit. Accessorise with colours like Dulux Wakefield to create an impression.

Perfect Browns – Mediterranean Harvest

Surround yourself in Dulux Mocha Magic to create a warm and inviting interior. Using this rich brown on the feature wall and scheming with Dulux Pale Oriental brings a fabulous balance between warm and cool colours. Pale Oriental is a yellow-green which goes beautifully with Mocha Magic to create a comforting overall scheme.

Polished style

Once seen as an economical alternative, polished concrete is fast becoming the ultimate in stylish, low-maintenance flooring. Because of recent advances in polishing equipment and techniques, concrete floor surfaces, whether new or old, can be ground to a high-gloss finish and stained with a variety of colours or imitated to look like polished stone. Factor in the superior durability and performance of concrete, and it is no wonder that polished concrete flooring has become **a considerable alternative** to marble, granite, tile, linoleum, or coated concrete. Recently homeowners have caught on to the appeal of polished concrete as it presents a hard-wearing flooring option, available with countless combinations of stones, pebbles, coloured oxide, glass, shell and marble. Specialist coatings and decorative cuts add to the eye-catching design possibilities for home flooring and concrete can also be a good choice for bench tops. Concrete floors are a durable and cost-effective option for both indoor and outdoor applications. Your individual choice of finish can flow through from kitchen to veranda, with non-slip honed finishes available for outdoor applications around pools and living areas.

Because polishing is a multi-step process, you can choose the level of sheen for your floors, from satin to high gloss polished concrete is easy to clean and maintain. With basic regular cleaning, the finish should keep its lustre for many years.

Coloured aggregate, glass, shells, pebbles or other objects can be added to the concrete mix or sprinkled into the top layer to create interesting and beautiful effects. The concrete is then shaped and polished, allowing kitchen bench tops, bathroom vanities, fire hearths and floors to be fully customised.

Interior inspiration - paint

Perfect Whites – Neutral Threads

For a touch of natural elegance, we have used Dulux Grand Piano as the Feature Wall in this lounge room. This colour highlights this wall very softly, without making a dramatic focal point within the space. Dulux Stowe White is the main colour throughout the room which adds a level of versatility and freedom to bring in other colours. Using colours in accessories like Dulux Crewelwork adds depth to the overall neutral colour scheme.

Perfect Greens – Finishing Touch

Greens are great for a soothing and relaxing feeling for any room. They are especially suited to living rooms, formal rooms and family areas. This colour scheme is utilising green (Dulux Bay Leaf) to give the room a cool, refreshed appeal and using a cooler colour combination can appear to make the room feel larger. Partnering Bay Leaf is the colour Light Ceramic, a softer green. Breaking up the greens with a different colour, Whisper White, on the Picture Rail, helps gives definition to the room and breaks up the two colours nicely.

Seaside inspiration

Set on the ocean's doorstep, this beachside home is perfectly designed to reflect its relaxing setting. The clean lines of the home and its minimalist décor work in harmony with the waterfront environment to create a year round holiday feel. Extensive use of pale timber throughout the home fitted perfectly with the owners' preference for natural materials. The natural look continues with deeper-coloured timber flooring laid inside and a lighter shade outside to enhance the indoor-outdoor flow. Sunlight bathes the lounge room during the day with large windows and glass doors framing sunrises and sunsets perfectly. Naturally, with a location such as this there is a desire to create the perfect alfresco area. Large decks at the back of the house provide this setting, only metres from the gentle, blue waves rolling onto Plimmerton Beach.

Interior inspiration - fabrics

By mixing any of Macrosuede's gorgeous decorator colours with a little flair and imagination, an interior can be transformed into a divine landscape - a chair awash in seafoam or marine and floor cubes or cushions rolled in storm and amethyst; or perhaps, a sensory feast - a sofa saturated in mulberry or port and placemats of saffron and basil adding subtle flavour to an intimate dinner. The beauty of Warwick's innovative new Macrosuede is in the contemporary fashion look it brings to any and every interior: the 58 brilliant colours inspired by nature's rich palette and the genuine suede-like texture that is heaven to caress combine with advanced durability to outsmart life's little reality checks. Once the sole domain of the high end of the market, this versatile manmade suede lends itself perfectly to the clean, straight lines of contemporary furniture and is now available to anyone sourcing quality interior fabric that is designed to last, despite the rigours of time, children, pets and parties.

Coastal inspiration

This superb family home embraces the coastal lifestyle with understated elegance, stunning views and the perfect environment for outdoor living. Its commanding position embraces the privileged Plimmerton lifestyle with relaxed class, unexpected space, tranquillity, security and best of all seclusion. Perhaps the most stunning features, the beautiful aqua coloured pool and extensive decking offer plenty of space to enjoy the views of the ocean and harbour from the privacy of your own personal oasis. Taking full advantage of the sea breezes and full sun, the established landscape is low maintenance and finishes the outdoor areas perfectly. Upon the hilltop, the home's views of the harbour are beautiful and extensive. The native forests and water ways surrounding Plimmerton make it an attractive destination and a great place to live.

Contemporary inspiration

This home perfectly contrasts bold, contemporary forms and natural materials creating a family home that reflects a seamless transition between the indoor and outdoor environments. Designed to be part of the same design experience the stone, marble and timber underline a strong connection between indoors and outdoors in this well designed home. Its fully fenced and the landscaped garden is designed to be an extended living area of the home. New Zealand's recent desire for an increasingly informal lifestyle continues to inspire homes that blur the boundaries between indoors and outdoors. To achieve this, a series of warm, comfortable living spaces are featured throughout the home maintaining a strong connection to the outdoors.

Inspirational views

With panoramic views out toward Mana Island and the South Island, this property is based adjacent to a native bush reserve and was built with quality of lifestyle in mind. Positioned on just over an acre, it is situated in one of the most sought after areas of Plimmerton in Wellington, accommodating and accentuating the breathtaking ocean views with walls of windows and large balconies.The natural surroundings of the coast and bushland are the perfect relief from city living, and it is positioned to enjoy all aspects of its location. With a balcony facing the shore and feature windows framing the native vegetation from all other angles, there are spectacular views no matter where you look. Its high ceilings and open plan allows natural sunlight to fill each living area and facing due north, the sunsets display a rainbow of colours which flood into the main lounge area. The double glazed windows and doors allow controlled amounts of sunlight to stream into the home.

Private Oasis

One of the potential drawbacks of living in a densely populated urban environment is the lack of privacy outdoors; however this home has managed to maintain an open and airy feel in the outdoor areas while sustaining seclusion. Located in a built up region of Buckland's Beach, the landscaping of the outdoor area consists almost entirely of a large swimming pool and surrounding decking. The walled yard allows sunlight to stream in with ease, yet upholds the privacy similar to that of a large acreage. The local climate is temperate, making year-round outdoor living a very real thing. Combined with efficient outdoor heating and the heated pool and spa, the back yard becomes a perfect small-scale piazza. The usability of the outdoor space is aided by the roof line of the building, which was designed to maximise the sunlight entering the courtyard and some of the home's interior spaces.

Beautifully designed and finished, this house offers perfection in its architectural layout, landscaping and furnishing. The finishes are contemporary in black leather, marble and grey slate surfaces. The attention to detail takes pride of place in all of the decorative characteristics of the home.

The state of the art kitchen is finished with the highest standard appliances and makes entertaining a pleasure. In keeping with the overall theme of the house, simple, minimalist lines are a feature of the kitchen. Opening directly onto the yard, the concealed nature of the house is a key to maintaining privacy in the space.

Interior inspiration - paint

Perfect Yellows – Elegant Appeal

To keep the lightness in this formal dining room we have used Dulux Tangent on the main walls, below the picture rail. This has given the room an overall warm and rich cream appeal. However, breaking up the colour of the walls, we have used Dulux Chalk U.S.A. which has given the sense of spaciousness and flexibility in accessorising. In this case we have used colours like Dulux Warm Neutral in the accessories, as the furniture in this room is quite dark and a lighter colour softens this a little.

The Dulux New Zealand Colour Map

The Dulux New Zealand Colour Map is a journey through more than one hundred New Zealand places and their colours. Colours that reflect the unique character of the country's most loved locations and most cherished settings. Timeless colours. From refreshing coastal blues to sombre volcanic greys, from striking alpine whites to tranquil bushclad greens. These are the colours we see all around us and all around the country. Think of the quietest town you've ever driven through or summer's best loved bach - and think of the colours that suit them best. You'll find them all in the Dulux New Zealand Colour Map. The Dulux New Zealand Colour Map comprises strongs, neutrals, brights and whites. As you look through it you'll find a brief description of each colour and suggestions for complementary "scheme colours". You can pick and choose any combination of colours because every colour in the map has been developed to sit with every other colour. You can team the far North with the deep South, Canterbury with Auckland, Fiordland with Hawkes Bay. Take a trip through the Dulux New Zealand Colour Map to arrive at the quintessential New Zealand colour scheme that will make you feel right at home.

Inspirational courtyard

Designed perfectly for its coastal location, this beautiful home invites alfresco living like no other. The huge bi-fold doors open to transform the main living area into two parts - indoor and out. The outside living area is fitted with an outdoor fireplace creating a relaxed, convivial atmosphere, which encourages you to linger long after the sun has set. This makes outdoor living an experience you can enjoy anytime of the year. The huge pool is well heated and is so large it almost covers the entire yard. Its bold, linear look mimics the clean lines of the minimalist home it is a part of. The atmosphere created by light-filled, open living spaces characterise this modernist home, which was designed to accommodate the ideal New Zealand lifestyle. The kitchen is a predominant feature, standing out from the timber trend of the home in light, lilac colours that continue to feature throughout the finishes of the home.

Tuscan dreams

This grand family residence proudly situated in sought after Fairfield Lane is an award winning Tuscan inspired masonry home, built to stand the test of time. With large wrought iron entry gates and an imposing appearance from the street, one cannot help but feel the true essence of one of Europe's strongest rural architectural traditions - the Tuscan Villa. Transplanted half the world away from Italy, the home has a sense of permanence and substantiality which contributes to the relaxed Tuscan-inspired lifestyle it offers. The clay tiled roof, heavy masonry construction and sandstone paving will all improve with age and the home's quality European fittings are evident throughout, including Italian porcelain flooring. Sophisticated and stylish, everything about this exceptional home is perfection. Landscaping that includes olive and lemon trees, an outdoor room and a patio with water features perfect the villa. Solid timber adds warmth to the home and accessories like wrought-iron furniture, drapery poles and sandstone paving complete the look.

Interior inspiration - fabrics

So bold and robust, yet so versatile. This is an innovation that's been worth waiting for. With Warwick's new Glam drapery range, the first thing that strikes you is the way the fabric captures the light of the space, creating a unique mood all of its own. There's an array of 55 dazzling colours in the selection – from hues of amber through to neutrals, and much deeper, darker tones. A fantastic artist's palette with which to go to work. Glam is a modern adaptation of silk, a taffeta fabric that is a 100% man-made yarn. Which means it's incredibly durable, stain-resistant, and the perfect compliment to any space that not only needs to look exceptional, but also lived in. It is well suited to everything from the contemporary loft to the traditional home and warms to open spaces and furniture with clean open lines. As a wall drapery, Glam accentuates the curves and rolls of hangings with a vibrant glow. In the evening sun one colour can become many as the light refracts around it, creating a remarkable soothing ambience.

Inspirational colours

Cast a glance down any New Zealand street. Chances are, every building will have been touched by Resene. Since its inception in 1946, Resene have forged an enviable reputation of excellence and quality in manufacturing products designed to meet the demanding standards of architectural and building industry professionals. Since its introduction of waterbased paint to a market starved of quality products in the 1950's, Resene have developed a range of paint and specialist coating products for residential buildings. **Many products have been developed as a creative answer to a client's problem**. New Zealand's harsh marine environment and high levels of damaging ultra violet rays quickly expose the limitations of overseas colour systems. As a result of this early discovery, the company developed a truly innovative Total Colour System based on sophisticated technology, to provide the necessary protection against the elements. When it comes to colour, **paint is about fashion**. Colours come and go with changing trends. Flexibility in colours, colour tools and colour scheme development is paramount. The company has embraced electronic imaging technology to convey colour and simplify the development and confirmation of colour schemes.

Detail, design and passion have culminated in a stunning Mt Maunganui home built on a down to earth budget and recognition as a Regional HOY Award winner. With a relatively small floor area of 184 square metres on a tight 400 square metre site to work with, the minimalist style engenders an air of spaciousness that belies the physical dimensions. Clad in Linea weatherboards and Titan Board, Linea was selected for its ability to be coated with dark Resene Bokara Grey (deep grey), unlike natural weatherboards that would be liable to warp due to the heat retention of the darker coating. Teamed with Titan Board and in-seal strips between panels finished in Resene Portland (mid grey) and a quarter strength of the same on soffits, the exterior oozes style. Lighting and colour are critical to mood and space. Resene Milk White (off white) from the Karen Walker range has been liberally applied throughout the entire home, then perceptually altered through the careful placement of lighting to cast shadows and draw out different elements of the colour. A sole splash of colour can be seen in the form of a Resene Domino (murky mid brown) feature wall behind the bed.

Wrapped in James Hardie Linea weatherboards, underpinned by a 'Pacific Rim' design philosophy and full of surprises behind every wall and in every storage area, the 'modpod' is an ingenious twist on the traditional kiwi bach. A key design challenge for this collaboration between Master Builders Haven NZ Ltd, Red Turtle Design and CTM Architectural was the restricted floor space - imposed by the intention to relocate the 'modpod' to Matarangi Beach Golf Estates following the Auckland Homeshow. This required a lightweight, flexible cladding system and timber flooring. The crisp linear aspect coated in Modpod Tope (Resene Half Pravda - sober beige) wraps into the house via an enclosed deck, with both weatherboards and decking continuing inside the main living area in a softer finish of Modpod Mini Tope (Resene Quarter Pravda). Warm contrast is delivered on exterior plaster using Modpod Mini Toto (Resene Fahrenheit - rich raisin red). Restricted space encouraged a focus on versatile functionality. Underpinning the unexpected spaciousness, the interior living area, laundry, halls, wardrobes and ceiling are completed in Modpod Echo (Resene Half Joanna - green toned neutral).

Taking advantage of popular hues, Resene Half Sisal dominates the interior, adorning ceilings, walls, architraves, skirtings and doors in varying sheen levels from full gloss Resene Enamacryl trims and joinery to Resene Zylone Sheen low sheen walls and Resene Zylone 20 flat finish ceilings. The variation in gloss levels provides visual stimulation in the restful atmosphere complemented by well toned features of Resene Tussock (strong yellow oxide) on the open plan living, dining and kitchen bulkhead wall, Resene Gingko (earthy neutral yellow) on the powder room/ensuite floating wall and topped off with a brave full gloss Resene Enamacryl splash of Resene Monza (bright red) on the front door.

The **food and wine** experience of New Zealand

Antoine's

Antoine's Restaurant has been the **leader in modern New Zealand cuisine** for over 30 years. The silver service restaurant has a unique and delicious menu heavy with French undertones and an extensive wine list. At Antoine's, Auckland's world class fresh produce is transformed into luscious dishes that are not only visually appealing, but also served with outstanding panaché. Opened in 1973 by Tony Astle and wife Beth, the restaurant seats up to 50 people and particularly caters for special occasion dining. Tony pays great **attention to all facets of grand cuisine**, beginning his culinary career at the age of 16 and training in Wellington at various upmarket restaurants. His philosophy of food today is a modern approach to cooking very much based on the techniques and heritage of great French cuisine. He cooks the freshest of New Zealand's produce, seeking out the best available ingredients. Tony's reputation as one of New Zealand's premier restaurateurs means that innovative, quality suppliers constantly contact him and willingly grow and supply product to his exacting specifications. Naturally, the high-class restaurant's **wine list is extensive** and hosts many New Zealand wines. However, as well as the local wines, the exceptional cellar at Antoine's also possesses French Bordeaux and Burgundy wines, which is much appreciated by regular clientele. With his excellent palate, Tony is New Zealand's leading chef at matching food and wine, and has a thorough knowledge of the New Zealand wine industry. Food and wine have exploded into New Zealand culture of late

and it is a fantastic thing. **Dining out a few times a week means that New Zealanders are beginning to expect higher quality wines and cuisine**. The restaurant, judged New Zealand's "Restaurant of the Year" 2003-2004, is located in the historic Parnell Village, Auckland's stylish haven of distinctive upmarket boutiques, galleries, restaurants, cafés and shops. This ideal location reflects Antoine's yesteryear quality service and its elegant residence in an historic villa. However, Tony is often invited to cook away from his restaurant, catering many parties and special occasions for private and corporate customers. He has cooked his distinctive fare in challenging situations as diverse as a businessmen's hunting expedition in the depths of rugged New Zealand bush country, to catering a weekend-long fortieth birthday bash for 100 guests on a private off shore island. He currently travels once or twice a year to top destinations in Asia, where he hosts special promotions in the very best hotels, featuring fine New Zealand food and wine in the famous Antoine's style. He has won many prestigious accolades and his cuisine is not to be missed. "**Our main goal is to make sure that our high standards of cuisine and service are maintained**. At the moment our good reputation precedes us and we would like it to stay that way" he says.

Antoine's

entree

Vine ripened tomato with buffalo mozzarella,
prawns and a citrus olive oil, and balsamic reduction.

6 medium vine ripened tomatoes
2 large buffalo mozzarella (fresh)

Dressing
300 mls extra virgin olive oil
30 mls lemon juice
1/4 tsp salt
1 clove crushed garlic
Place all ingredients in a bottle, shake well.

Prawns
18 shelled prawn tails (Green) uncooked
1 litre water
1 1/2 tablespoons salt 1 1/2 tablespoons sugar (Brine)

Bring water, salt and sugar to the boil. Drop in the prawns. Stir with slotted spoon. Remove when just cooked, and drop into iced water to chill. Drain and keep chilled.

Balsamic Reduction
200 mls Balsamic vinegar
Pour into small pot. Bring to boil and reduce by half. Remove from heat and cool to create a syrup.

To Serve
Slice the tomato into 5 even slices leaving the calyx (green stalk)
Slice the mozzarella, carefully
Between each slice of tomato, place a slice of mozzarella
Place 3 prawn tails on each
Decorate with chiffonade of basil plus a head of basil
Drizzle with the well shaken olive oil dressing.
Finish with a little balsamic reduction.

Serves 6

Antoine's

main course

Squid Ink Risotto with Tempura Oysters

Squid ink risotto, kina and caviar cream
1 tablespoon olive oil
1 1/2 cups Arborio rice
1/4 cup dry white wine
5 cups chicken stock (hot)
1 packet squid ink (or tbsp)
4 tablespoons grated fresh parmesan
2 tablespoons unsalted butter
1/2 tablespoon truffle oil
salt and pepper to taste

In a large saucepan, heat the oil over medium heat, add the rice. Stir to coat, and sauté for 3 minutes.

Add the wine and simmer stirring occasionally until the liquid has been absorbed.

Add half the stock and simmer,stirring occasionally until the liquid has been absorbed.

Add the remaining stock and squid ink, stirring until rice is cooked el dente

Remove from heat and incorporate cheese, truffle oil and butter.

Season and keep warm.

Serves 6

Sails

Set in the heart of the huge Westhaven Marina, the views from Sails Restaurant are filled with the sails of thousands of yachts, **capturing the essence of the city of Auckland** and providing the perfect backdrop for a first class dining experience. This serene sight is complimented by the supreme range of seafood the restaurant offers, from traditional Fish and Chips to Shahjira Dusted Snapper or Cured Akaroa Salmon Tartlets. "When dealing with quality produce the less you do to it, the better. With **years of experience in overseas kitchens in Austria and England**, Sails' executive chef has an understanding of food from all cuisines and believes that the most important ingredients are the talents of the chefs and an excellent range of fresh food. "If you employ the best chefs and ensure they have access to only the freshest top quality ingredients the result will be award winning dishes" he says. This is made easy in Auckland with endless supplies of high quality fresh produce from its markets and oceans. Many fruit and vegetable farms throughout the area surrounding the city provide its restaurants with a great selection of fresh greens and herbs. Additionally, weekend markets at Otara and Avondale offer Asian, Indian, Pacific Island and European fruit and vegetables, alongside fresh seafood. Because of this, **Sails has received a multitude of awards** including being judged three times as one of the best restaurants in New Zealand. Jason Blackie has also received awards for his food served at Sails. He was declared the overall winner at Nelson's annual seafood festival, 'Hooked on Seafood'. The competition invited 120 established restaurants

from around the country to enter into a competition to create New Zealand's best seafood dish. The four finalists then went down to Nelson for the final cook off, where Jason was crowned the winner being awarded the title of 'National Supreme Seafood Chef'. Sails' also have one of New Zealand's most extensive wine lists, including **rare vintages from New Zealand's top vineyards**. The cellar style list focuses predominantly on wine from local vineyards but also includes renowned Australian and French wines. The restaurant can comfortably seat up to 130 people, still leaving the bar area available for pre-dinner drinks, mingling or dancing if needed. Larger numbers can be accommodated for cocktail parties or if the bar area is used for tables. Sails is only minutes from Downtown Auckland but a world away from traffic jams and parking hassles as there is free parking for more than 150 guests right outside the door. With a setting and backdrop as spectacular as the views of the marina, Harbour Bridge and Rangitoto Island, Sails is the perfect place to unwind and truly comprehend the spirit of Auckland.

Sails

entree

Pan Seared Prawn Tails with soba noodles and coconut dressing

20 raw prawn tails, peeled and deveined (entree size for four people)
Marinade lightly with 3tsp olive oil, 2 cloves of crushed garlic,
a little fresh chilli and 2 tsp of chopped coriander.

The Salad
100g cooked soba noodles, julienne of carrot, daikon, cucumber, pickled ginger,
toasted pinenuts, coriander, mint leaves, spinach leaves and fresh pineapple.
Mix together the above ingredients with some coconut dressing.
Place equal amounts of salad onto four plates.
In a very hot pan, sear your prawns and place on and around the salad.
Drizzle more of the coconut dressing onto the plate
Serve immediately

Coconut Dressing
300 ml coconut cream
2 stalks of lemon grass
60 g palm sugar, grated
60 mls fish sauce
2 tsp sambal (chilli paste)
60 mls lime juice

Method:

Bring the coconut cream, lemongrass, palm sugar and fish sauce to the boil in a saucepan uncovered.

Reduce to a simmer and stir in the chilli paste and lime leaves.

Taste and adjust seasoning

Serves 4

Sails

main course

Grilled Yellow Fin Tuna with roasted vine tomatoes, scallion, avocado, and Spanish olive oil dressing

4 pieces of yellow fin tuna (or any game fish 170g per portion)
12 vine tomatoes, drizzled with olive oil, sea salt and oven roasted for 6 mins on 180ºc
4 scallion trimmed, blanched and lightly grilled
avocado salsa – 1 avacado, peeled and diced, 1tsp lemon juice, salt/pepper,
fresh coriander and a dash of tabasco.
Spanish olive oil dressing

All can be done in advance except the cooking of the fish which should be done at the last minute.

Assembly
Place three vine tomatoes in the centre of each plate followed by the scallion and tuna. Drizzle over the fish a generous amount of the Spanish olive oil dressing and a spoonful of avocado salsa.

Pickling juice
1/2 cup water	1 tsp mustard seeds
95 ml rice vinegar	1 tsp black peppercorns
95 g sugar	1 tsp ginger, chopped
1 tsp kosher salt	1/2 tsp chilli, seeded and chopped
1 clove	

Method for Pickling Juice
Combine all of the ingredients in a small saucepan and bring to a simmer,
allowing the salt and sugar to dissolve.
Cool and use as needed.

Spanish olive dressing
1 cup red onion, sliced
2 tsp grape seed oil
1 cup pickling juice
1 tsp each chopped coriander and sage
80 ml olive oil
1 cup sliced olives

Method for Spanish Olive Oil Dressing
In a small saucepan, sauté the red onion in the grape seed oil until translucent.
Add 1 cup of pickling juice and continue to cook for three minutes.
Remove the pan from the heat and let it stand in the pickling juice for one hour.
Strain and reserve both the onions and the pickling juice.
Place the reserved pickling juice in a small bowl.
Add the herbs and slowly whisk in the olive oil.
Add sliced olives, season to taste with salt and pepper.

Serves 4

Grand Chateau

The Mount Ruapehu Grand Chateau is one of the most luxurious hotels in New Zealand and amongst the most unique in the world. Located within the Chateau, **The Ruapehu Restaurant** is not unlike the hotel it belongs to. With a traditional mouth watering and body warming menu, it is the perfect place to dine on cold winter nights, only minutes from the ski fields. Flanked by the volcano of Mt Ngauruhoe on one side, the snowy peaks of Mt Ruapehu on the other, diners are provided with views that are almost as good as the food. The restaurant's namesake, Mt Ruapehu, is New Zealand's highest volcano reaching 2797 metres which also makes it the highest mountain in the North Island. This snowy mountain has erupted about 50 times since 1861, with the most recent major eruption occurring in 1975. At the top of the volcano there is an acidic crater lake, which thousands visit every year. The Ruapehu restaurant resides far enough away to view the beautiful volcano from a much safer distance. Renowned for its classical styling and grandeur, The Grand Chateau opened in 1929 and retains its timeless elegance. The building itself is one of New Zealand's most famous and over the years, its facilities have been constantly updated to enhance many of its most endearing original features. It is also the only Hotel located in the Tongariro National Park. **Walking into the Grand Chateau is like stepping back in time**. Guests still drive up a ramp to alight at the hotel's front door under a portico. Inside, huge windows frame views of beech forest and Mt Ngauruhoe. Crystal chandeliers glitter above cosy armchairs and roaring log fires, a grand piano, a billiard table and a parquetry dance floor. The dining room and interiors are furnished in mahogany, walnut and New Zealand ash helping the building to retain the glamour, luxury and high standards of service of its time. So far, about $10 million has been spent on refurbishing the hotel in keeping with its registration as a Category 1 historic place. The Chateau and the Ruapehu Restaurant not only offer the perfect escape during chilled winter months but also the perfect escape from the rush of the 21st Century.

Vintage Wine

New Zealand has long been renowned for its natural beauty and exotic landscape, but more recently its wine has been soaking up the international acclaim. Over the past ten years the wineries of New Zealand have produced some of the finest wines in the world. Regions such as Hawke's Bay, Marlborough, Auckland and Canterbury offer perfect climates and soils to produce near perfect vintages. The country of vast contrasts also has considerably different wine regions, suitable for different wines. With wine growing regions spanning the latitudes of 36 to 45 degrees and covering the length of 1,600 kilometres, grapes are grown in an extensive range of climates and soil types, producing a diverse array of styles. The coastal vineyards, such as those near Hawke's Bay and Auckland have a strongly influential maritime climate. The vines are warmed by strong, clear sunlight during the day and cooled at night by sea breezes. The long, slow ripening period helps to retain the vivid varietal flavours of the wines and produce a unique aroma. To coincide with New Zealand's love of food, the wines produced here are intended to be savoured with fine cuisine. Inspiration from the traditional kitchens of France and Italy, as well as the exotic dishes of Asia and the Pacific Rim have produced a wide range of cuisines that suit the strong taste of New Zealand wines. Our wine styles have evolved to compliment this extensive menu with zesty wines such as Sauvignon Blanc and Riesling for the spicy dishes of Asia, while smooth Chardonnay and Pinot Noir offer a timeless union with the more classical dishes of Europe. The joy of wine does not only come from its savouring, but also the visiting of the vineyards where locals and visitors can taste a selection of wine and experience the true beauty of viticulture. Wine tours are available countrywide and are usually only an hour away from most major cities. New Zealand's relationship with wine may be younger than that of Italy and France, but it promises to be just as significant.

Herzog

When Hans and Therese Herzog opened their winery in 1999, they knew they would need a **brilliant restaurant** that could serve simple yet tasty cuisine to accompany their full flavoured wines. That is why they imported one of the leading chefs from their winery in Switzerland with them on their journey to New Zealand. Head Chef Louis Schindler now runs this fine restaurant with a dedicated European team. The Herzogs come from a winegrowing heritage that dates back to 1482. Driven by a desire to grow perfect wines, they moved their renowned winery and Michelin-starred restaurant from their native Switzerland into the heart of Marlborough where they have become established as **one of New Zealand's leading boutique estates**. Herzog Luxury Restaurant maintains its European influence with Mediterranean inspirations and a simple yet stylistic menu. The focus is on fresh ingredients, full flavour and a perfect wine match. The restaurant was built out of pure passion, giving locals and visitors to New Zealand the opportunity to experience the Herzog wines with world-class food – as they were intended. Open from October to May, the restaurant offers exquisite five and three course menus, featuring Herzog's own wines, as well as an award-winning wine list extending over 500 wines. French silver cutlery and finest china, crystal glasses and a professional yet unobtrusive service enhances the dining experience. Another unique aspect of Herzog Winery and Restaurant is its size.

At only 30 acres, the winery is **a European style vineyard** with a huge variance in wines for such a small acreage. Herzog Winery and Restaurant also have Masterclasses teaching members of the public the secrets of fine cuisine. These are a great opportunity for novices and food enthusiasts to work with top European Michelin star-experienced chefs while having fun learning about fresh market cuisine. They are **'hands-on' workshops** offering an opportunity to learn about the preparation and presentation of a 3-course menu that can easily be put into practice when entertaining at home. For a truly unique experience, there is 'Kitchen Confidential' which is an ultimate behind-the-scenes insight into the running of a gourmet kitchen. With a maximum of two guests per class, the experience includes the observation of the running of the kitchen, preparation of the food, finished with a three course meal and range of wines to taste. Even when the Herzogs began their winery in Switzerland in 1986, they knew that New Zealand was the place they wanted to end up. They visited the country in the early 1980s and after travelling the world looking for vineyard properties, they fell in love with the New Zealand lifestyle and its endless opportunities.

Sileni

Sileni's Restaurant, set in the large winery estate of the same name, is charmingly nestled between vineyards in Hawke's Bay on the east coast of the North Island of New Zealand. Offering supreme culinary standards, **a visit to the Sileni Estate is a total food and wine experience**. Inspired by Mediterranean cuisine and using only the freshest local produce, the restaurant dedicates itself to developing a regional cuisine that fits the local wines and achieving natural, simple, but strong flavours and textures. From its inception in 1998, the Sileni vision was to build a very strong culinary image around its wine, with a gourmet food store, restaurant, culinary school, wine education centre and a food and wine reference library onsite. Head Chef Jenny Parton believes that the foundation of such delicious dishes is the range and quality of the fresh local produce. The quality of the restaurant experience is enhanced by the combination of appetising meals with the superb wine list that showcases not only Sileni wines but also the best of Hawke's Bay, New Zealand and the World, especially those based on Merlot, the flagship variety of Sileni. It is this reputation for excellence that ensures the restaurant is almost always full, especially during the popular summer months. The food and wine experience Sileni offers is not restricted to the sampling of such diverse tastes, but there is also a **culinary school** which teaches classes to cook the fine cuisine and delicacies that the restaurant offers. Classes are flexible and at convenient times for participants at all levels. The class is mostly made up of locals as it runs fortnightly from April to December.

Sileni Estates was one of the first vineyards established in Hawke's Bay, which offers a perfect climate for producing world-class fine wines that achieve international acclaim. Situated in an area of the country renowned for its agricultural excellence, **Sileni Estate has a climate similar to that of some of the great wine regions of France**. Located on a coastal plain, it is one of the best soils for viticulture as alluvial gravel are free-draining and warm, providing natural conditions to prevent excess vigour and to allow the development of concentrated, ripe flavours in the grapes. The Sileni wines are based on classic Old World styles, with the advantage of New Zealand's intense fruit flavours providing pleasant palettes. At full production, Sileni will make some **80,000 cases of wine** from current plantings on 100 hectares of vineyards in Hawke's Bay. The Sileni Estates multi-million dollar investment reflects the confidence that owner and Chairman Graeme Avery has in the climate and agricultural excellence of Hawke's Bay, and his belief that the region will also become New Zealand's premier wine and food tourism destination. Sileni Estates is delivering a gratifying experience to its visitors and Graeme's intentions are clear "Our mission is to make New Zealand's best world class wine".

Sileni

entree

Salmon Ceviche on Cucumber & Pickled Ginger Salad, with Soy & Lime Dressing & Topped with Wasabi Flying Fish Roe

Ingredients
1 x salmon fillet
1 x red onion
2 x coriander plants
2 x lemons (zested on grater)

Method
Remove brown meat & pinbones from fillet. Slice salmon fillet into 4 mm strips
Dice red onion, chop coriander, zest lemon over a bowl, add salmon and mix thorough
ingredients.Toss through the following dressing and leave to marinate for 20 minutes before
serving.

Soy & Lime Dressing
400 gr brown sugar   100 ml fish Sauce
400 ml sweet mirin   4 tsp pickled ginger
200 ml soy sauce   4 x onions – chopped
200 ml white wine vinegar   1 tsp oyster sauce
200 ml fresh lemon juice   1/2 cup coriander root

Method
Combine all ingredients and simmer over a low heat for one hour.
Pass through a fine sieve and refrigerate.

Cucumber & Pickled Ginger Salad
1 x telegraph cucumber
1 tsp toasted sesame seeds
1/4 cup pickled ginger

Method
Cut cucumber in half lengthways and scoop out the seeds with a spoon.
Leave the shin on and mandolin into noodles.
Finely chop the pickled ginger and mix through the toasted sesame seeds.
Season & serve immediately.

To Serve
Place a small amount of salad in a porcelain spoon
Lay 2-3 slices of salmon on top
Top with wasabi tobiko & hijiki.

Sileni Estates Wine Match: Estate Selection 'The Lodge' Chardonnay

Pegasus Bay

For Chris and Ivan Donaldson, a life long passion for wine blossomed into a life changing and agreeable vocation they are still enjoying over ten years after they opened the cellar doors at the Pegasus Bay Winery. "Since we became of a drinking age, we fell in love with wine. It has so much variety and so many different facets. Not only does it taste divine and help form friendships, it is has many health benefits" Chris says. Her husband, Professor Ivan Donaldson, has **promoted the health benefits of wine** throughout his dual careers as viticulturist and medical professional. His distinguished career in medicine was closely followed by his pioneering career in wine. The couple started in 1967 with small-scale winemaking which eventually led to the planting, with partners in 1976, of the first vineyard in cool climate Canterbury, which is only just above the 44th parallel. Their burgeoning interest in wine led to the establishment of Pegasus Bay Vineyard and Winery at Waipara in 1985, where eldest son Matthew, Roseworthy oenology and viticultural graduate, is now winemaker, with his wife Lynnette. Pinot Noir specialists, their wines are now exported to northern markets in small quantities. "There are over 140 scientifically proven health benefits from drinking wine. Especially for the heart and blood as it lowers cholesterol. It has also recently been proven to help with Alzheimer's" says Chris. The aim at Pegasus Winery is to **grow grapes of the highest quality**, which fully express the features of the vineyard, and to handle these with the utmost respect. Using natural methods and as little intervention as possible at all stages from vine to bottle typifies their approach.

Within the Waipara Valley, Pegasus Bay Vineyard gets maximum protection from the Pacific's easterly breezes by being tucked up under the lee of the Teviotdale range. Heat summation during the day is promoted by smooth stones and gravels left behind by an ice age glacier. The soil is freely draining and of low fertility, resulting in naturally reduced vine vigour. Another important aspect of the winery is its **high quality restaurant**. From inception, the winery planned to focus on both wine and food as the Donaldsons believe that both are equally important to attain the full experience. "From day one we planned to include a restaurant, as soon as the cellar doors opened so did the restaurant's doors," she adds. Since opening in 1992, the restaurant has changed locations at various times as the winery has grown. It is now based in a beautiful setting designed for both indoor and alfresco seating. The family believe that food and wine matching is very important and emphasise this in their restaurant. "Visitors can see the difference in a family owned and run place and I think it is obvious in the amount of passion and care we express."

style

Contacts

Pages

10-21 Woodlot Properties   Web: **www.woodlotproperties.co.nz**

22-25 Purple South   Web: **www.purplesouth.com**

26-29 Mayfair Pools   Web: **www.mayfairpools.co.nz**

30-39 New Work Studio   Web: **www.newworkstudio.co.nz**

40,100,120 Warwick Fabrics   Web: **www.warwick.co.nz**

42-45 Studio of Landscape Architecture   Web: **www.landscapearchitect.co.nz**

46-53 The Fireplace   Web: **www.thefireplace.co.nz**

54-59 Untouched World   Web: **www.untouchedworld.com**

60-63 Cavalli Beach House   Web: **www.cavallibeachhouse.com**

64-65 Polynesian Spa   Web: **www.polynesianspa.co.nz**

66-67 The Pillars Retreat   Web: **www.pillarshomestay.co.nz**

68-69 L'Unova medi-spa   Web: **www.lunova.co.nz**

70-71 Fitzroy Yachts   Web: **www.fitzroyyachts.co.nz**

72-89 Don Nelson & Associates   Web: **www.donnelsonarchitecture.co.nz**

90, 96, 114 Dulux   Web: **www.dulux.co.nz**

92-95 Polished Concrete   Web: **www.polishedconcrete.co.nz**

98,99,1102,103,104,105,106,107 Open2view – Rob Arlow   Web: **www.open2view.com**

108-113, 116-119 Open2view – Elise Burridge   Web: **www.open2view.com**

122-129 Resene   Web: **www.resene.co.nz**

132-139 Antonie's Restaurant   Web: **www.antoinesrestaurant.co.nz**

140-147 Sails Restaurant   Web: **www.sailsrestaurant.com**

148-149 Grand Chateau   Web: **www.chateau.co.nz**

152-155 Herzog   Web: **www.herzog.co.nz**

156-159 Sileni Wines   Web: **www.silini.co.nz**

164-167 Pegasus Bay   Web: **www.pegasusbay.com**